GOI WHOSE POWER IS LOVE

Group study and reflection for Lent

MICHAEL FORSTER

kevin mayhew

First published in 2005 by

KEVIN MAYHEW LTD
Buxhall, Stowmarket, Suffolk, IP14 3BW
E-mail: info@kevinmayhew.com
www.kevinmayhew.com

9 8 7 6 5 4 3 2 1 0

ISBN 1 84417 492 1
Catalogue No. 1500860

Cover design by Angela Selfe
Edited and typeset by Katherine Laidler

Printed and bound in Great Britain

Contents

To the memory of my big sister, Elizabeth
with thanks to God for a life well lived and well loved

Foreword

I'm writing this book to introduce the God who's been with me over some pretty eventful decades; together we've gone through an incredible childhood – surrounded by amazing love, but struggling to find myself nonetheless – followed by all the uncertainty and conflict of teenage years when I was deciding which image I thought the world would like me to clothe myself with. We've shared the unspeakable joys and the terrible tears that my relationships with others have brought – my amazing wife who loves me as much when I'm a liability as when I'm helpful; our son who gave us eight lovely years and taught us so much before he died; a whole host of other people who have inspired, tested, delighted and infuriated me along the way.

Throughout a sixty-year search for my own self, God has never left me, even though I can sometimes be a pretty tough companion to have around. He's not been an easy companion himself, mind you. He's got this annoying habit of treating me like an adult – even when I don't feel like one, which is most of the time. Sometimes I just want to be led – to be told where to go, what's the right decision to make; I just want to *know* that what I'm doing is right. Not that much to ask, is it? I ask him what his plan for my life is, and he sort of shrugs and says, 'Don't *you* want to have some say in that?' Sometimes he adds some irritating philosophical remark about being 'open to the future' and 'trusting the process'. It's almost as if he doesn't have a 'plan' at all – or not in that sense, anyway – but just a whole lot of confidence that wherever we go together he'll be able to hack it. That's all very well, but it's not always what I want.

I wouldn't swap him, though. We laugh together, we cry together – and when I completely lose it with him and say some seriously unchristian things to him, he takes it; no thunderbolts, no dire consequences – but occasionally I catch just a glimpse of a kind of deep, deep sadness. Not that he parades it manipulatively, don't get me wrong, but in my better, more sensitive moments, I see it.

That's another time I wish he'd use his power – put right whatever it is I've done, rub it out as if it had never happened – but he doesn't, because he reckons life without consequences would just be meaningless. Oh, no, I don't get off the hook that easily – which is sort of OK, I guess, because it means that what I do matters. There again, though, he doesn't hold grudges. After all the let-downs, rebellions and downright mind-blowing stupidity, he's still there – right with me when I want him to be, but ready to fade into the background when I'm daft enough to think I don't want him around.

Well, I could go on, but maybe you get the picture. This is my God – my companion God of sixty years now – and this is my chance to introduce him to you.

MICHAEL FORSTER

About this course

What we believe about God matters enormously; it affects not only our conscious processes but more importantly our unconscious motivations and attitudes. Following and serving a God who controls, manipulates and overrides individual freedom is a very different matter from journeying with a God who sacrifices power in the interests of building meaningful relationships and accepts willingly the suffering that that entails.

The question is not about whether or not God has power – that goes without saying – but about what God *does* with that power. Is power something to be exercised over others to get our own way, or a resource to be shared so that together we can have meaningful lives and relationships? Day by day, all of us have decisions to make about how to use our power – whether at work, in our families, or our social environments. Do our exchanges with others tend to empower them or control them?

We do not need to reflect for very long to come to a radical conclusion: exercising power does not build relationships – sharing it does. That's scary, because sharing power means making ourselves vulnerable – trusting that others won't abuse the share we give them. That's why some people consciously choose not to engage in relationships, either withdrawing into hermit-like lifestyles or adopting aggressive or manipulative attitudes that keep them in control.

The Christian belief is that that's God's dilemma too; and the cross is the ultimate price paid by an empowering and power-sharing God intent upon building meaningful relationships with creation at whatever cost necessary to himself.

The aim of this course is actually to experience some of the issues this raises, so there is no designated 'leader'. Clearly, someone will need to act as a *facilitator*, enabling the process to happen, but that person must resist at all costs any pressure to become a decision-maker, arbiter or director. When that pressure is felt, a good way to handle it is to focus attention on how the group is feeling, and what the need to be led is about at that moment. Is this how we are with God? Is God trying to share power with us who prefer to put it back on to him along with all the responsibility?

It will also be important to recognise that some people may find the ideas challenging, even threatening, and a strong source of pastoral support should be available to the group(s), during and between sessions.

The course may be used with one group of people (if necessary breaking into smaller groups for discussions) or perhaps by a number of separate house groups simultaneously.

Five weeks is a good length for a Lent course. However, given the nature of the material, some churches may prefer to have some specific reflection upon the cross. So I have added a shorter supplementary session that could be used during Holy Week if desired.

Suggested framework for a session

Opening devotions

We could argue that the entire session is 'devotional' – God can speak to us even through the most powerful disagreement and conflict! So you might prefer to substitute this opening with something else. Just keep it brief and simple; possibly listening to some reflective music from Taizé or Iona. Margaret Rizza's work includes some very suitable material.

Experiential group work

We begin from our own experience, and then reflect upon that in the light of Scripture. This may seem the reverse of some traditional approaches, but teachers know that learning is best achieved if we start with something familiar, moving from the known to the unknown, rather than first trying to grasp a new idea from cold.

One vital point to remember is that people's experience is their experience. Others might have interpreted it differently, or responded in other ways, but the story belongs to the teller – so treat it with respect even it if raises questions for others.

Main Bible study

A short Bible passage focuses attention upon an aspect of what we believe about God. The Bible passage is printed here to provide a common starting point. While reading it, it will be important to try and set aside traditional assumptions about these familiar texts, and be open to what new things might emerge in the light of different people's experiences.

Reflection/discussion

Remember: the idea is not to engage in learned exegesis, but to ask what this passage says to us in the light of our *experience*. No two people's experiencing is the same, even of the same event, so everyone's contribution is valuable. It will, though, demand openness to being challenged about some traditional ideas. If what we've always believed doesn't seem to sit well with our experience, there are radical questions to be asked – and this course is designed to help us not to duck them!

While doing that, awareness of feelings is important. If something seems to make sense but we still struggle to accept it, then let's pay attention to how we're feeling about it. Is the idea threatening? Is it asking questions we've been taught not to ask? Does it relate to how we like to view ourselves? Sensitive, experienced pastoral care must be available as part of the course's structure.

Don't be afraid of silence. Far from indicating that the discussion is over, it may mean that much internal processing is going on. Maybe the discussion will resume and take a new direction, or perhaps ideas are being carefully stored away for processing later.

Optional additional material

If it becomes clear that the discussion of the main material *has* been exhausted and some new impetus is needed – or if it just seems like a natural progression – then you might like to include this extra material. It is designed to provoke further thought and perhaps move the discussion on, but should not be used as a deflection when the discussion is getting challenging!

Refreshments

Very important – time to socialise and unconsciously work on those all-important personal relationships. If we are considering the idea that God prefers to work through relationship, then time spent informally (and very probably unconsciously) building those between ourselves is part of the learning and reflective process.

It will be important that people are encouraged not to continue the discussion in this period. Sometimes ideas gel better if we leave them alone rather than constantly stir them up. This time is for friendship, not for debate. A way of facilitating this might be to jot down a few interesting news items to mention, and casually begin conversation before the group breaks. That way, the evening's discussion may not be not the only thing in their minds as they relax.

Worship preparation

Exactly how this is used will depend on whether there is just this one group meeting or others – perhaps as house groups. If the former, then there's no reason not to use the time to develop some kind of presentation; if the latter, then it might be just a matter of focusing on one point from each group.

So, bearing that in mind, what would the group most want to say to the congregation on Sunday?

You won't be able to say everything – so this is an exercise in trusting God, each other and the worship co-ordinator who will pull the threads together during the service! Often a simple thought, condensed into a few words, will send people home thoughtful and open – we can trust God for the rest!

Session 1
A power-sharing God

A God who shares power with us, rather than using it for us, can be a scary concept. It's not unnatural to want someone to lead us, take our decisions and the responsibility that goes with them; that's one of the struggles we all had in our growing-up experiences: we wanted to be called adults, but weren't always quite so keen to take the responsibilities that went with that!

This first session calls upon the whole group to share the responsibility of decision-making and leadership. How will that feel?

As this is the first session of the course, it might be helpful to set the tone – before formally beginning – by asking people to read (or having one person read aloud) the Foreword on page 5.

Opening devotions

Light a candle in the middle of the space, the people grouped around it.

Silence

Meditation – read by one of the group

> We light a candle to remind us of the presence of God, the Light of the World, in our midst.
>
> We cannot look at the candle without seeing each other, grouped around it.
>
> And we cannot look across at one another without being aware of the light.

So may it be that the more we seek God, the more aware we become of each other;

and as we listen to each other more deeply, may we encounter more fully the divine presence within and between us.

Silence

Experiential group work

Spend a few minutes thinking about what sort of group you want to be.

Should you appoint a leader? If so, how would you see the leader's role?

- Control/steer discussion?
- Settle arguments?
- Arbitrate?
- Silence heresy?
- Enable participation?
- Smooth over differences?
- Make people feel better?
- etc.

Does this reflect what we expect of God? Does the idea of a God who refuses to control us – preferring to enable us to take responsibility – scare us a little?

I hope you won't appoint a leader, but rather allow a suitably skilled person to *facilitate* the discussions. Whichever you do, keep in touch with how you're feeling about that decision – and how it has affected the group – as the weeks go by.

Main Bible study: 1 Samuel 8:1-22

When Samuel became old, he made his sons judges over Israel. The name of his firstborn son was Joel, and the name of his second, Abijah; they were judges in Beer-sheba. Yet his sons did not follow in his ways, but turned aside after gain; they took bribes and perverted justice.

Then all the elders of Israel gathered together and came to Samuel at Ramah, and said to him, 'You are old and your sons do not follow in your ways; appoint for us, then, a king to govern us, like other nations.' But the thing displeased Samuel when they said, 'Give us a king to govern us.' Samuel prayed to the LORD, and the LORD said to Samuel, 'Listen to the voice of the people in all that they say to you; for they have not rejected you, but they have rejected me from being king over them. Just as they have done to me, from the day I brought them up out of Egypt to this day, forsaking me and serving other gods, so also they are doing to you. Now then, listen to their voice; only – you shall solemnly warn them, and show them the ways of the king who shall reign over them.'

So Samuel reported all the words of the LORD to the people who were asking him for a king. He said, 'These will be the ways of the king who will reign over you: he will take your sons and appoint them to his chariots and to be his horsemen, and to run before his chariots; and he will appoint for himself commanders of thousands and commanders of fifties, and some to plough his ground and to reap his harvest, and to make his implements of war and the equipment of his chariots. He will take your daughters to be perfumers and cooks and bakers. He will take the best of your fields and vineyards and olive orchards and give them to his courtiers. He will take one-tenth of your grain and of your vineyards and give it to his officers and his courtiers. He will take your male and female slaves, and the best of your cattle and donkeys, and put them to his work. He will take one-tenth of your flocks, and you shall be his slaves. And in that day you will cry out because of your king, whom you have chosen for yourselves; but the LORD will not answer you in that day.'

But the people refused to listen to the voice of Samuel; they said, 'No! but we are determined to have a king over us, so that we also may be like other nations, and that our king may govern us and go out before us and fight our battles.' When Samuel had heard all the words of the people, he repeated them in the ears of the LORD. The LORD said to Samuel, 'Listen to their voice and set a king over them.' Samuel then said to the people of Israel, 'Each of you return home.'

Reflection/discussion

This is a really interesting and revealing passage! The people wanted a king so that they could be like all the other nations – but, of course, the whole perception of themselves as a chosen people meant that they were *not* like everyone else! Why did they want a king? There's a strong whiff of buck-passing here: the king will govern them – tell them what's right, settle their arguments, make their decisions, all that kind of thing – and he will also go out and fight their battles for them.

Could it be that God would rather share power with us than exercise it over us – but we keep trying to hand it back because we can't hack the responsibility? Do we want God to solve our problems, rather than empower us to deal with things ourselves? Remember how it felt at the beginning of the session: was there a desire to be 'led' rather than trust the group process?

How are people feeling now? Is the idea of a power-sharing God an attractive one – or a scary one?

Optional additional material

Bible reading: Romans 13:1-7

Let every person be subject to the governing authorities; for there is no authority except from God, and those authorities that exist have been instituted by God. Therefore whoever resists authority resists what God has appointed, and those who resist will incur judgement. For rulers are not a terror to good conduct, but to bad. Do you wish to have no fear of the authority? Then do what is good, and you will receive its approval; for it is God's servant for your good. But if you do what is wrong, you should be afraid, for the authority does not bear the sword in vain! It is the servant of God to execute wrath on the wrongdoer. Therefore one must be subject, not only because of wrath but also because of conscience. For the same reason you also pay taxes, for the authorities are God's servants, busy with this very thing. Pay to all what is due to them – taxes to whom taxes are due, revenue to whom revenue is due, respect to whom respect is due, honour to whom honour is due.

Reflection

Why did Paul write this? Is he really saying that the regimes of, for example, Adolf Hitler and, more recently, Saddam Hussein were divinely sanctioned? Were the people who were afraid of them really the guilty ones?

This and similar passages have served well those Christians who have chosen to ignore rather than oppose injustice (often, to be fair, in fear for their own and their families' lives). Paul himself clearly was not afraid to oppose authority – including that of the apostle Peter himself – and probably died a martyr at the hands of the Roman Emperor.

Or, since Paul clearly expected the imminent end of the world, was he simply trying to keep the peace, avoid creating unnecessary turmoil, and let Christians focus on preparing to meet their Maker?

Without getting into the political issues just now (important though these are, they aren't the purpose of this course), consider the connecions between the two readings. Is there a deep-seated human desire to pass responsibility on to leaders rather than shoulder it ourselves?

Before the discussion ends for refreshments, it would be good to take some silent time together, closing with someone reading Psalm 23, with this introduction:

> This is a psalm of confidence in God's presence and ultimate trustworthiness. The psalmist firmly believes God will be with him in the dark valley, but – and this is immensely significant – he does not expect God to rescue him from it, but rather accompany him through it, with the assurance that together they will find the new life beyond.

Refreshments

Worship preparation

Think about how worship happens in your church. Is it down to one person to take most or all of the responsibility? Does that person tend to get the blame if it isn't to everyone's liking?

How about the group sharing responsibility for the service?

How could the customary 'leader' become an enabler, a facilitator, instead?

One example might be to offer at one point in the service a choice of hymns; try and get a discussion going as part of the choosing process, and then reflect afterwards how it felt to the congregation to be involved in that decision. Some will approve, but others may resent the imposition and say that that's the job of the worship leader.

That's one possibility – can you think of others?

Would this be acceptable?

Session 2
Power and relationships

Today we're going to look at how God tries to move the relationship on from one based on his power and control to one founded upon unconditional love.

Opening devotions

Light the candle

Silence

Meditation – read by one of the group

> We are here as a lawless group – we have no rules to govern us.
>
> Each of us relies entirely on the kindness of the others – as all the others rely on each of us.
>
> This makes us different; in the world, group work always involves ground rules – rules that everyone agrees to keep – about respect, about honesty, about consideration, about confidentiality.
>
> We don't have any – because we hope we don't need them. That's what makes us different from the world.
>
> We're a lawless group.
>
> Or rather, perhaps, a law-free group.
>
> A society of grace.
>
> Thanks be to God!

Silence

Experiential group work

Let's say we're worried about the rise in disputes between neighbours in society generally – more and more, petty arguments are turning into vendettas and serious damage is done. We need to nip it in the bud. So let's campaign for a new law. We'll call it 'Rule 11': 'Thou shalt not offend thy neighbour.'

That should put a stop to it at source – anyone who offends their neighbour will be prosecuted, so they won't dare, will they?

Now, as a group, discuss the practicalities of this. Many questions should arise, for example:

How, in legal terms, do we define 'neighbour'? Next door? Next door but three? Across the road? On the world-wide web?

What constitutes 'offending' one?

- Swearing?
  What words are swearwords? Do we need an exhaustive list?
- Telling him he smells when he doesn't?
- Telling him he smells when he does?
- Playing loud music?
  Should decibel meters be fitted by law on all hi-fi equipment?
  What about someone practising the trumpet?
  Who decides what's 'good' and what's 'bad' noise?

Just those few issues – let alone the rest that the group may think of – will probably make it seem pretty impractical. This is not a new discovery. You might find it significant that while the Ten Commandments take up 16 verses (Exodus 20:2-17), the book of Leviticus has 859 verses – and that's just *one* of the law books!

No one's suggesting that all laws are unnecessary – but are we expecting too much of them? What other ways are there of handling neighbourly relations?

Main Bible study: Matthew 5:21-48

Jesus gets to the true heart of the law

Jesus gives some examples of how true faithfulness means going beyond mere legalism. The question for him is not, 'What does the law literally say?' but 'What is its true purpose and intention?' The examples take the form of six 'antitheses' which begin with words such as 'You've heard what used to be said' and go on to 'But *I'm* telling you . . .'

You've heard what used to be said to people, way back: 'Don't commit murder' – and anyone who does will be liable to the judgement of the courts? Yes, well, that's fine as far as it goes, but *I'm* telling you that even giving in to the anger underlying it will make you liable – to the judgement of God himself. You go round insulting one another and you'll be held to account – and throwing around insults like 'Idiot!' will put you in danger of hell itself. So next time you're getting ready for worship, and you remember that someone's got a grievance against you, go to them first – get right with them, and then you can think about worshipping God. Setting relationships right isn't something you can just keep putting off. Someone suing you for something? Settle out of court before it all runs away with you and you find yourself banged up for it – because there'll be no half measures then, and you'll end up paying the full penalty.

You've heard what used to be said: 'An eye for an eye and a tooth for a tooth?'* Well, again, that's fine as far as it goes, but *I'm* telling you, you can't even go that far. Don't be always insisting on your individual rights, defending your own property, as though those things were what mattered. If someone gives you a backhander to your right cheek, well, offer them your left one, too. Someone wants to sue you for your shirt? Be generous! Give

* In the Law of Moses, this was a limit not a licence – the *absolute maximum* allowed, intended to stop the excesses that had led to blood feuds.

your jacket as well – it's worth more! And next time some jumped-up tin soldier forces you to carry his pack for a mile, well, show him what civilisation really is, and carry it for two! Beggars? Don't be selfish – give to them. And if someone asks to borrow something, don't come out with pious excuses – share a bit!

You've heard what they used to say: 'Love your friends' – which seems to imply that you should hate your enemies. But *I'm* telling you: love your enemies; pray for people who have a go at you. This is so that you can truly be children of your Father in heaven who doesn't have any favourites at all. Doesn't he send sunshine to bad people as well as good, rain to both faithful and unfaithful? I mean, what's so special about loving people who love you – anyone can do that. Even the tax gatherers are canny enough to stick together!* And if you only speak to people who're the same as you, what makes you different from anyone else? Even outsiders do that.

In other words, your example of true goodness should be God, your heavenly Father – model yourselves on him!

Reflection/discussion

Is our constant inclination towards legalism a sign of insecurity? Do we find it hard to trust ourselves and one another?

Do we prefer a powerful God who makes and enforces laws to a vulnerable one who wants us to build free relationships and work on our difficulties together?

Optional additional material

Bible reading: Romans 12:9-21

Marks of the True Christian

Let love be genuine; hate what is evil, hold fast to what is good; love one another with mutual affection; outdo one another in

* Jews gathering taxes for the Roman occupiers were despised by their fellow Israelites.

showing honour. Do not lag in zeal, be ardent in spirit, serve the Lord. Rejoice in hope, be patient in suffering, persevere in prayer. Contribute to the needs of the saints; extend hospitality to strangers.

Bless those who persecute you; bless and do not curse them. Rejoice with those who rejoice, weep with those who weep. Live in harmony with one another; do not be haughty, but associate with the lowly; do not claim to be wiser than you are. Do not repay anyone evil for evil, but take thought for what is noble in the sight of all. If it is possible, so far as it depends on you, live peaceably with all. Beloved, never avenge yourselves, but leave room for the wrath of God; for it is written, 'Vengeance is mine, I will repay, says the Lord.' No, 'if your enemies are hungry, feed them; if they are thirsty, give them something to drink; for by doing this you will heap burning coals on their heads.' Do not be overcome by evil, but overcome evil with good.

Reflection

When people who think they are 'good' or have a 'good cause' wage war against 'bad' people and causes, and win, has good overcome evil? Or have 'good' people simply adopted evil ways on the basis that ends justify means?

Might it not then be said that evil (as distinct from evil *people*) has won?

In calling us to overcome evil with good, is Paul not really saying that we should refuse to be dragged into evil ways, even if that costs us dearly?

Is that not an important aspect of the 'victory of the cross'?

Refreshments

Worship preparation

Think about the general tone of worship services. Do people usually go away feeling they need to improve, or celebrating being loved as they are? What can we do this Sunday to make our worship more grace- and less works-centred?

Session 3
Power of love confronts love of power

Opening devotions

Light the candle

Silence

Meditation – read by one of the group

> This is good.
>
> We're comfortable here – in [*Name*]'s home – and in the presence of God.
>
> We know we're welcome – in [*Name*]'s home – and in the presence of God.
>
> Each of us matters – no one is more important than another, just because they're older or younger, male or female, working, unemployed or retired.
>
> Not even because they happen to own the place!
>
> Because [*Name*] has made us all equally welcome.
>
> God makes us welcome.
>
> Thanks be to God for his unfathomable grace!

Silence

Experiential group work

Think about places where people would feel ill at ease. Some people might be overawed in a university building or in a law-court; many would feel intimidated going into a celebrity's home, while some others find banks scary. When I began in the NHS as a chaplain, I was afraid to go into the nurses' office on the ward in case it was felt I shouldn't be there!

So, how overawed would *we* be in the presence of God if we were really fully aware of it? Would we want to keep a low profile in the hope we weren't noticed, or would we hold our heads high as people who, *by the grace of God*, have a right to be there?

Main Bible study: Luke 13:10-17

An oppressed woman in the synagogue

A healing miracle, yes – but so much more besides! Wholeness involves more than the healing of physical ailments (no matter how serious they in themselves may be). When Jesus enables the woman to stand up straight – hold her head up, we might say – in the synagogue, he tells her not that she is 'healed', but that she is 'freed from her oppression'. He also calls her a 'daughter of Abraham' – a remarkable dignifying of womanhood for that time. These clues point to a deeper meaning that we are invited to grasp.

One Sabbath day Jesus was teaching in the synagogue when a woman came in who'd been oppressed for eighteen years: she couldn't stand up straight. Jesus noticed her straightaway, of course, and called her over to him. 'Lady,' he said, 'you're free from all that oppression, as of right now.' He reached out and touched her. Her back straightened, her head came up and she looked everybody in the eye. Well, she started praising God as she'd never praised him before!

As you'd expect, the man in charge of the synagogue wasn't so happy. According to him, Jesus shouldn't have done the healing because it was the Sabbath when no one's allowed to work. So he announced to all the crowd, 'Look, there are six perfectly good days in every week when it's legal to work. So, if you want healing, you come on one of those days – not on the Sabbath. Got it?'

Jesus had an answer for him. 'Oh, you absolute hypocrite!' he said. 'Don't you take care of your animals on the Sabbath – untie them, lead them to water? So, why shouldn't this woman – a descendant of Abraham, and don't you forget it – who's been oppressed by evil for all these years – why shouldn't she be set free from the oppression on the Sabbath day?' Well, that put the opposition in their place! They were hugely embarrassed, of course – but the whole crowd was ecstatic, because of the terrific things he was doing.

Reflection

I'm getting less and less happy with the traditional 'non-conformist prayer hunch' where we curl ourselves forwards as if trying to get our heads as low as possible like the courtiers in *The King and I*. God is not a vertically challenged potentate who feels insecure in the presence of bigger people! Similarly – I am now convinced – he does not want me to feel obliged to make myself small in his presence. God thought that a good relationship with me was something to die for! I matter! So I now hold my head up when I pray; not in arrogant defiance, but in grateful – and gracious – acceptance of the relationship that God, by grace, is offering me.

What does this reading say about God and the kind of relationship he wants with all people?

Is that the image most people have?

If not, why not – and what can we do about it?

Optional additional material

Bible reading: Leviticus 21:16-23

The LORD spoke to Moses, saying: Speak to Aaron and say: No one of your offspring throughout their generations who has a blemish may approach to offer the food of his God. For no one who has a blemish shall draw near, one who is blind or lame, or one who has a mutilated face or a limb too long, or one who has a broken foot or a broken hand, or a hunchback, or a dwarf, or a man with a blemish in his eyes or an itching disease or scabs or crushed testicles. No descendant of Aaron the priest who has a blemish shall come near to offer the LORD's offerings by fire; since he has a blemish, he shall not come near to offer the food of his God. He may eat the food of his God, of the most holy as well as of the holy. But he shall not come near the curtain or approach the altar, because he has a blemish, that he may not profane my sanctuaries; for I am the LORD; I sanctify them.

Reflection

This is one of those terribly inconvenient passages that really force us to put our understanding of the authority of Scripture on the line!

Do we really believe that God spoke these words – and, if so, are they valid for all time?

Or dare we think that this is an example of some very human writers sanctifying their own fears and prejudices?

We could argue that a God who sacrifices power for relationship would not have simply erased such material from Scripture, but left it for us to interpret with the help of his Spirit – and hopefully to learn from!

Is our desire for a God of power partly to do with justifying our own prejudices and particularities?

Refreshments

Worship preparation

Go back to the opening discussions and think of 'unchurched' people coming to worship. Might they feel overawed or intimidated? At Anstey URC, they once had to come into a completely enclosed porch first, and then pluck up the courage to open the door and venture into the unknown. We put a window in the porch so that the entire church was visible from there and suddenly it seemed a whole lot less intimidating – especially if there were already a few 'regulars' visible, laughing and joking inside!

Ask the question: 'What kind of God does the building – and the experience of worship – seem to represent?' and consider how that question could be raised with the worshipping congregation.

Session 4
To be truly great is to love

Opening devotions

The candle is lit

Silence

Meditation – read by a group member

> We meet in the presence of God, the Light of the World.
>
> The candle flame *offers* us its light – it does not force it upon us like a halogen floodlight. As we immerse ourselves in our discussions, we could easily forget that it's there.
>
> The flame is not protected. It flickers in any momentary draught.
>
> Any one of us could reach forward and snuff it out.
>
> Is this how God approaches us? Humbly and unthreateningly – open to our rejection or abuse?
>
> Do we see that as weakness or as greatness?

Silence

Experiential group work

Who are the people whom the group members have valued – the ones who told them what to do, or the ones who listened, cared and, when necessary, rolled their sleeves up and helped?

Have one or two examples ready to get the ball rolling, and encourage the group to share their own experiences – but be careful not to let anyone feel pressurised to disclose things they are not happy to share.

My own example might be the couple who came and sat with us all night after a sudden death. They couldn't change the event that had happened, and they didn't have any smart answers to our questions or balm for our anger. But as long as we needed company they were there. They were among the truly great people we have known.

Here's a story about some people who wanted 'greatness' but probably weren't expecting it to take this form.

Main Bible study: Mark 10:35-45

The disciples jockeying for position

Then James and John, Zebedee's sons, came to Jesus. 'Teacher,' they said, 'we'd like you to do something for us.'

'Oh, yes?' Jesus answered.

'Can you, sort of, well, promise that we'll be the top guys alongside you in your kingdom?'

Jesus said, 'You really don't have any idea what you're asking, do you? I mean, have you got the stomach to drink from the cup that I'm soon going to have to drink from?* Can you go through my baptism?'

'What? Oh, that – oh, sure!' James and John answered.

'Well,' Jesus told them, 'drink my cup you certainly will – and go through my baptism, too – but to have the top places in my kingdom, well, that's not mine to give. That's not something you can aspire to or earn – it's a gift of God.'

When the word got round, the other ten were hopping mad

---

* The 'cup of suffering' would be a familiar metaphor to any Jew, and Jesus is trying yet again to get it into the disciples' heads that his route to glory is through suffering. He'll still be trying to do that when he acts out this idea at the Last Supper – and they still won't be getting it!

with James and John, but Jesus called them to him and spelt it out yet again. 'Look,' he said, 'you know how it is in the old order of things: kings on thrones giving orders to everyone else, bullies having all the clout – a proper rat-race – well, you'd better get it into your heads that it's not going to be like that among you. One of you wants to be thought of as great? Fine, then be a good servant to all the rest. And if you want to be put first, then you'll need to be like a slave, just like the Son of Man who didn't come to be waited on but to serve others, and to pay the cost of human freedom with his own life!'

Reflection

Is this a bullies' charter? In my mental health work I meet many vulnerable people who are encouraged to 'serve' by others who have a vested interest in it.

There are great dangers in an overly simplistic use of this text. So how can it be used creatively?

How do we value those who for one reason or another find it difficult to 'serve' in the usual ways. Is there a 'service' (as Milton famously suggested) in just being around?

Is that what our friends were doing that night – just being there?

We often long for a God who will intervene and solve our problems (as long as he solves the ones we want him to, of course . . .).

Does the cross show us a God who transforms things by 'just being there'?

That question could occupy some groups for years on end – but here's some additional material, anyway!

Optional additional material

Bible reading: John 13:1-17

As the Passover festival approached, Jesus knew that the time had come – soon he was to leave this world and go to the Father. He'd always loved the ones who'd been his friends in the world – and he loved them to the end. Judas, son of Simon Iscariot, was already harbouring sinister intentions – the devil was really getting at him to betray Jesus.

Jesus washes his disciples' feet

> Some people think it rather mysterious that Jesus waited until the meal had started before washing his disciples' feet. It should strictly speaking have been done on their arrival, and certainly before the food was served. Various reasons have been put forward for this, but I must say that it seems pretty obvious to me. The meal itself was a community event – it was also a symbol of the kingdom of God. Of course, Jesus wanted to make as close a link as possible between the community meal and the principle of service: 'This is the kind of community you must be: sharing life – the whole of life – together (symbolised by food and drink) and humbly serving each other (shown in the foot washing).'

During the supper Jesus knew what a moment this was – the Father had entrusted him with everything; he'd come from God, and now he was gong back to God. He got up from the table, stripped off his tunic and wrapped a towel round his waist. Then he poured some water into a bowl and proceeded to go round the table washing his disciples' feet and carefully wiping them dry on the towel.

As he approached Simon Peter, Simon protested, 'What's this – *you're* surely not planning on washing *my* feet, are you?'

'I know it looks odd now, but one day you'll understand,' Jesus assured him.

'Oh, no!' Peter was adamant. 'I'm not having that! Never! Absolutely out of the question!'

'OK,' said Jesus, 'so you don't want me to wash you – that means that you don't have anything to do with me or what I'm about. If that's what you want . . .'

'Oh! Right, well, that puts a totally different complexion on it, doesn't it! Look, why not do my hands and my head as well, while you're at it!'

'You're missing the point, Peter,' Jesus told him. 'You've already had a bath – right? So you just need your feet washed after the walk. That's because you're basically clean. And you all *are* clean, aren't you?* – well, actually, not *all* of you are.' He knew, of course, which of them it was that was about to betray him – and that's why he said, 'Not *all* of you are clean'.

After he'd washed their feet, got dressed again and gone back to his place at the table, he said:

> Have you any idea what I've *really* done for you just now? I mean, you call me things like 'Teacher' and 'Lord', right? And that's fine, because that's exactly what I am. OK, then – so if I – Lord, Teacher and all that stuff – have just knelt on the floor washing your feet, then you might just get the point that I'm expecting you to do the same for each other – because I've just given you an example to follow – a pattern – do as I've done. I'm really telling you straight: slaves aren't greater than their masters, are they? – people who carry messages aren't superior to the ones who send them out, are they? If you know that – well, congratulations are in order if you do it too!

---

* I've added the 'all' here to show that the 'you' is plural. Jesus is talking about the group of disciples, not just Peter. As always, we must remember that this is very symbolic stuff: Jesus wants his disciples to think about something deeper than just having dust-free feet!

Reflection

Peter found the humility of Jesus offensive. He was supposed to be the leader – the Big Cheese! Three rather different thoughts occur:

1. Do we find relating to a God who doesn't fit our stereotypes difficult? We know where we stand with the 'power and might' stuff, but where does this place us?
2. Does a powerful God appeal better to our insecurities than a humble one? Is there a part of us that wants to be protected, and gets jumpy when we are treated as autonomous adults?
3. Does being servants of a powerful God have more kudos about it than being servants of a humble one? Many of us have a need for power, status, recognition – even if we don't particularly like it in ourselves. Does a humble God challenge us too deeply, perhaps?

Refreshments

Worship preparation

Think about the intercessions. What are you going to be asking God to do? Does it seem appropriate to ask God to do things, or might it be more a matter of recognising his humble presence in people's lives and praying that we shall be open to that and allow ourselves to be changed by it?

The way we pray – particularly in intercession – says a great deal about the kind of God we believe in. So what do you really want to say?

Session 5
The saving power of love

Opening devotions

If you can find them, place a model or picture of a medieval knight on a warhorse, and one of a farmyard donkey, on the table by the lighted candle.

Silence

Meditation – read by a group member

> In the face of our demand for a king, a knight-rescuer, God seeks to be King of our hearts – but only on the basis of our willing acceptance of him.
>
> The King approaches – riding a derisory donkey and armed only with love and the willingness to suffer.
>
> When God does this, it is no act – no empty gesture. It is done the way God does everything – with complete integrity and absolute openness to the consequences.
>
> Are we ready to accept the offer?
>
> Are we open even to recognise it for what it is?
>
> Or shall we try to change it into something we like better?

Silence

Experiential group work

How has it felt over the past few weeks, not having a 'leader'? Or have you, perhaps, appointed one anyway?

Has one just 'emerged', and been tacitly accepted by the group with a sense of inward relief?

Or have the past weeks been an experience of shared power – of co-operative learning, rather than being taught?

I have twice experienced higher-education courses run on person-centred lines, in which the tutors have invited us to share their learning journey rather than merely sit and be taught. We were expected actively to learn, rather than passively soak up the wisdom of the staff. Ultimately, we found this approach immensely stimulating – and the learning so much deeper and more effective. But most of us, initially, shared in a feeling of being 'let down' – even accusing the tutors of ducking their responsibilities. We'd come here to be taught – why would they not just do what we were paying them for?

Does any of this feel familiar to the group?

Main Bible study: Mark 11:1-11

They were approaching Bethphage and Bethany at the Mount of Olives within sight of Jerusalem. 'Right,' Jesus said to two of his disciples, 'I'd like you to go into the village, and immediately you get there you'll find a colt tied up – one that's never been ridden. Just untie it and bring it to me here. Oh, and if anyone says, "What are you two up to?" just say, "The Lord needs it and he'll return it immediately."'

The disciples went off on their errand and found the colt tied up outside a door, right on the street. As they untied it, the people around said, 'Hey! What do you think you're up to, untying that colt?' But as soon as the disciples told them what Jesus had said, they stopped arguing about it and let them go.

Jesus enters the city

So they brought the colt to Jesus, and threw their own coats over its back – well, it was the closest they could get to ceremonial livery, and it looked dead impressive, even if a little bizarre – and Jesus sat on the colt to ride into town. Everybody got in on the act – talk about putting out the red carpet! Some of them used their own coats, while others cut foliage from the fields to put on the road. They were a real sight: crowds in front of Jesus, crowds following behind him, all shouting, 'Saviour!* Son of David!' and joining in the traditional festal chant, 'Congratulations to the one who's coming in God's name!' Then they added, 'Blessed is the coming kingdom of David, our father! Praise God in the highest!'

Jesus himself got to Jerusalem and went to the Temple, but when he'd had a look round it was getting late and he went back to Bethany with the Twelve.

Reflection

This is often called the 'Triumphal Entry'. In using that term are we buying in to the false expectations of the crowd? It's pretty clear they were expecting a liberator – a rescuer – who would 'lead them to victory'. Does this have echoes of the first session and the people's demand for a king? Remember how God warned them that the king they wanted would not be good for them, but they ignored him?

I sense a huge battle of wills going on here, as Jesus offers the people a final chance to get the message – accept him as a 'King of hearts', not as a powerful overlord – while the rabble-rousers determinedly cast him in the mould of their rescuer.

Is this why the crowd were so easily swayed the other way within the week?

Is this the disappointment clients often feel when a counsellor 'fails' to solve their problems but instead tries to support and empower them?

---

* The word 'Hosanna' literally means 'Save us', but had come to be used as a shout of praise more than as a prayer in itself. Here the crowd are praising Jesus *as* Saviour.

Is this why we constantly seek a powerful God, and often only pay lip service to the weakness and vulnerability he chooses?

Optional additional material

Bible reading: John 18:33 – 19:6

So Pilate went back into his headquarters and sent for Jesus. 'Am I supposed to believe that *you* are the King of the Jews?'

'Is that you speaking?' Jesus asked him. 'Or are you just repeating what someone else has said?'

'Oh, get real – I'm not a Jew, am I! Look, your own people – your own chief priests have dumped you on me, so what did you do for either of us to deserve that?'

Jesus answered, 'My kingship bears no relationship to what this world understands by that term. I mean, if it did, my servants would be fighting for me, wouldn't they, to stop me being handed over to the authorities? But my kingship's about something quite different from that.'

'Oh,' Pilate countered, 'so you clearly *are* a king, then?'

'It's you that say I'm a king,' Jesus replied. 'The real reason I've been born, and come into the world, is to testify to truth. Anyone who's on the side of truth listens to my voice.'

'What *is* truth?' Pilate shrugged.

After saying this, he went back out to where the religious authorities were waiting, and said, 'I find no case against this man at all, but let's compromise. You know that custom you have, that I release a prisoner for you at Passover time – how about I release this "King of the Jews" character?'

There was absolute uproar! 'Not on your life – we don't want this guy at any price! Give us Barabbas!' Now, Barabbas was a rebel.

Jesus is mocked

Then Pilate sent Jesus for a merciless flogging. That wasn't enough for the soldiers, though: they literally added insult to injury – wove a crown from thorns and put it on his head, and dressed him in a purple robe. Then they kept coming up to him, saying, 'Hail, O King of the Jews!'* and slapping him.

Pilate went outside again. 'Look,' he said, 'I'm bringing him out here and I want you to be in no doubt about it – I don't find anything against the guy.' So Jesus came out, complete with the crown of thorns and purple robe. 'There,' Pilate said. 'Look at the man!'

As soon as the chief priests and Temple police set eyes on him, they started yelling hysterically, 'Crucify him! Crucify him!'

Reflection

Pilate is clearly relishing the chance to mock the Jews – is this really the best they can do for a king? The cross is still offensive to many people of faith who cannot bring themselves to believe that God would weaken and demean himself to allow such treatment. Perhaps the response of the priests and Temple police is not so alien to us if we're really honest?

Can we accept a God who is so determined to have a relationship with us that he has chosen to be this vulnerable, this weak, this undignified?

Refreshments

Worship preparation

Is there, at the heart of our traditional Palm Sunday celebrations, a revealing flaw? God comes to us in vulnerable humility, seeking a way into our hearts, and we give him the welcome reserved for a conquering hero, a political rescuer!

Without suggesting that we overturn the whole Palm Sunday tradition at a stroke, is there something else we want to say in our worship this time?

---

* This is irony: Jesus *is* the King, but in a very different sense, and the mockery will ultimately be turned back upon themselves.

Supplementary material: The cross – the power of suffering love

Opening devotions

Place a cross – or better, a crucifix – beside the lighted candle.

Silence

Meditation – read by a group member

> There is power here.
>
> Not the power to topple thrones and empires,
> not the power to push rockets into space,
> not even the power to boil a kettle!
>
> No, this is a different power:
> the power to change hearts and minds;
> the power to turn away anger,
> the power to turn fear into compassion,
> hatred or callous indifference into love,
> and endless streams of words into awestruck silence.
>
> Behold the power – and the glory – of God.

Silence

Experiential group work

Does anyone know the origin of the common handshake? Most of us probably use it at least once a day, but never stop to think about its significance.

It originated in days when people fairly commonly carried swords, and was a sign of trust in that one cannot shake hands while holding a weapon (like many traditions it catered for the right-handed majority, of course!).

In the Scouting movement, the handshake is done with the left hand; I'm told that this originates from old military traditions, since it is necessary to put down one's shield.

So is some degree of vulnerability a necessary and unavoidable part of building good relationships?

Does this also apply to God – or does he have a secret magic formula we know nothing about?

Bible Study: Mark 15:22-39

They took Jesus to the place called 'Golgotha' (which means 'the place of the skull') and offered him a mixture of wine and myrrh to drink, but he wouldn't accept it. Then they crucified him and divided up his clothes among themselves by gambling for them to decide what each of them was going to get out of it. This was about nine in the morning. The placard over his head read, 'The King of the Jews!' They crucified two rebels with him, one either side. People who passed by ridiculed him, shaking their heads and saying, 'OK, then – you who reckoned you could destroy the Temple and rebuild it in three days – you can start by saving yourself – just step down from the cross – surely you can do a little thing like that!' All the chief priests joined in mocking him, too. 'He saved others,' they jeered, 'but he can't save himself, can he! Oh, come on – he's the king of Israel – so let him just come down from the cross – seeing's believing, after all!' Even the rebels, crucified on either side, joined in and taunted him.

The death of Christ

At midday there was a horrible darkness everywhere. It lasted until three o'clock in the afternoon. And at three, Jesus gave a great and terrible cry. 'My God,' he screamed, 'my God – why have you deserted me?'

Some of the people said, 'Hey, listen to that! He's calling Elijah.' One kind person ran over to where the soldiers were sitting, soaked a sponge in their wine and held it up on a stick for Jesus to drink, saying, 'Let's just wait and see whether Elijah will come to save him!'

Then Jesus gave another great cry, and breathed his last.

At that precise moment, the curtain that hid the holy of holies in the Temple was ripped in two from top to bottom. When the centurion who was standing facing him saw how he died, he said, 'Surely it must be true that this is the Son of God!'

Reflection

The curtain is torn – the truth of God is displayed for the world to see.

But what is this 'truth'?

Here's a powerful reflection on that famous question.*

> I learned recently that the Greek word for truth is *alētheia* the prefix *'a'* meaning 'not'. What 'is not' is *lēthē.* You might think this word mean 'lies' or 'falsehood', but its meaning is 'oblivion'. The opposite of truth is oblivion. The opposite of truth is about annihilation, hiddenness, forgetfulness, unconsciousness and non-existence.
>
> I imagine Christ as one whose life is mercilessly taken, and yet also given. He gave his living and he gave his life to and for a cause, the truth . . . the truth of human experience at the margins, the truth of the poor, the truth of women, the truth of the 'unclean', the truth of the abused, the truth of children, of people with disability, of people who didn't fit or whose mental pain could not be heard.

* I'm indebted to my friend and colleague, Revd Dr Jo Harding, minister of Grove Lane Baptist Church, Cheadle Hulme, for this reflection.

> He gave his living and his life to raising their reality from oblivion and into the light, into visibility. He gave his living and his life to taking their experience of injustice out of oblivion and into significance and resistance. He risked his own life rather than allow the truth to go unspoken and for their lives to pass without acknowledgement, and he identified the presence and solidarity of God with the resistance and protest that marked his way of being in the world.
>
> And so in the silent 'scream' of the cross we hear truth. In the powerlessness and anguish of the cross we see injustice exposed. In the violence of the cross we find the protest of God against *every* act of violence and violation, against every false definition, against every stolen voice and hope, which would mean oblivion for its victim.
>
> Thus God's non-violent scream of protest will not fade while others will take it up, 'take up the cross' and follow on.

There is life-transforming, world-changing power here.

The power of God whose power is love.